More praise for *Simple Passion*

"Abundantly wise . . . In her inimitable spare prose, Ernaux—like a medieval anatomist bent on finding the soul—dissects a love affair to discover the point of passion. . . . A stunning story . . . that pulsates with the very passion Ernaux so truthfully describes."

—*Kirkus Reviews*

"*Simple Passion*'s strength lies in its unblinking examination of the emotional netherworld of obsession . . . Ernaux captures perfectly the delicate longing of it . . . *Simple Passion* is scrupulously unsentimental, exposing not so much the narrator's emotions as the *phenomenon* of those emotions, the way they have taken over her life."

—*Los Angeles Reader*

"Ernaux, one of France's bestselling and most controversial writers, writes with a spare and intense elegance. . . . Ernaux eschews romance; she records no expectations, no delusions. This is, instead, a documentation of pure sexual passion, a verbal diagram of the narcosis of desire."

—*Booklist*

SIMPLE PASSION

Simple Passion

Annie Ernaux
Translated by Tanya Leslie

Ballantine Books • New York

English translation copyright © 1993 by Quartet Books
All rights reserved under International and Pan-American Copyright Conventions. Published in the United States by Ballantine Books, a division of Random House, Inc., New York, and distributed in Canada by Random House of Canada Limited, Toronto. Originally published in France by Éditions Gallimard in 1991.
Copyright © 1991 by Éditions Gallimard

This edition published by arrangement with Four Walls Eight Windows

Library of Congress Catalog Card Number: 94-94286

ISBN: 0-345-38254-4

Cover design by Georgia Morrissey
Cover art detail of C. W. Eckerberg's *Woman Before a Mirror*, circa 1837. Courtesy of the Hirschprung Collection, Copenhagen

Manufactured in the United States of America

10 9 8 7 6 5 4

SIMPLE PASSION

Nous deux – le magazine – est plus
obscène que Sade

ROLAND BARTHES

This summer, for the first time, I watched an X-rated film on Canal Plus. My television set doesn't have a decoder; the images on the screen were blurred, the words replaced by strange sound effects, hissing and babbling, a different sort of language, soft and continuous. One could make out the figure of a woman in a corset and stockings, and a man. The story was incomprehensible; it was impossible to predict any of their actions or movements. The man walked up to the woman. There was a close-up of the woman's genitals, clearly visible among the shimmerings of the screen, then of the man's penis, fully erect, sliding into the woman's vagina. For a long time this coming

[1]

and going of the two sex organs was shown from several angles. The cock reappeared, in the man's hand, and the sperm spilled on to the woman's belly. No doubt one gets used to such a sight; the first time is shattering. Centuries and centuries, hundreds of generations have gone by, and it is only now that one can see this – a man's penis and a woman's vagina coming together, the sperm – something one could barely take in without dying has become as easy to watch as a handshake.

It occurred to me that writing should also aim for that – the impression conveyed by sexual intercourse, a feeling of anxiety and stupefaction, a suspension of moral judgement.

[2]

From September last year, I did nothing else but wait for a man: for him to call me and come round to my place. I would go to the supermarket, the cinema, take my clothes to the dry cleaner's, read books and mark essays. I behaved exactly the same way as before but without the long-standing familiarity of these actions I would have found it impossible to do so, except at the cost of a tremendous effort. It was when I spoke that I realized I was acting instinctively. Words, sentences, and even my laugh, formed on my lips without my actually thinking about it or wanting it. In fact I have only vague memories of the things I did, the films I saw, the people I met. I behaved in an

[3]

artificial manner. The only actions involving willpower, desire and what I take to be human intelligence (planning, weighing the pros and cons, assessing consequences) were all related to this man:

> reading newspaper articles about his
>   country (he was a foreigner)
> choosing clothes and make-up
>   writing letters to him
> changing the sheets on the bed and
>   arranging flowers in the bedroom
> jotting down something that might
>   interest him, to tell him next time we
>   met
> buying whisky, fruit and various
>   delicacies for our evening together
> imagining in which room we would
>   make love when he arrived.

In the course of conversation, the only subjects that escaped my indifference were those related to this man, his work, the country he came from and the places he'd been to.

[4]

The person speaking to me had no idea that my sudden interest in their conversation had nothing to do with their description or even the subject itself, but with the fact that one day, ten years before I met him, A had been sent to Havana on an assignment and may have set foot in that very night club, the 'Fiorendito', which they were describing in minute detail, encouraged by my attentive listening. In the same way, when I was reading, the sentences which made me pause were those concerning a relationship between a man and a woman. I felt that they could teach me something about A and that they lent credibility to the things I wished to believe. For instance, reading in Vassili Grossman's *Life and Fate* that 'people in love kiss with their eyes closed' led me to believe that A loved me since that was the way he kissed me. After that passage, the rest of the book returned to being what everything else had been to me for a whole year – a means of filling in time between two meetings.

I had no future other than the telephone call fixing our next appointment. I would try to leave the house as little as possible except for professional reasons (naturally, he knew my working hours), forever fearing that he might call during my absence. I would also avoid using the vacuum cleaner or the hairdryer as they would have prevented me from hearing the sound of the telephone. Every time it rang, I was consumed with hope, which usually only lasted the time it took me slowly to pick up the receiver and say hello. When I realized it wasn't him, I felt so utterly dejected that I began to loathe the person who was on the line. As soon as I heard A's voice, my long, painful wait, invariably tinged with jealousy, dissipated so quickly that I felt I had been mad and had suddenly become sane again. I was struck by the insignificance of that voice and the exaggerated importance it had taken in my life.

If he told me he was arriving in a hour – 'an opportunity', in other words an excuse to be late without arousing his wife's suspicions – I would enter a different phase of waiting, devoid of thought or even desire (to the extent of wondering whether I would be able to achieve an orgasm), bursting with frenzied energy, unable to organize the simplest tasks: having a shower, getting out the glasses, painting my nails, mopping the floor. I no longer even knew who I was waiting for. I was entirely at the mercy of that crucial moment when I would hear the car brake, the door slam and his footsteps on the concrete porch – a moment which I always anticipated with unspeakable terror.

When he left me more time between his phone call and his visit, three or four days, I imagined with disgust all the work I would have to do and the social engagements I would have to attend before seeing him again. I would have liked to have done nothing else but wait for him. I lived with the growing obsession that something might happen to stop us from meeting. One afternoon, when I was driving home and expecting him half an hour later, it occurred to me fleetingly that I could have an accident. Immediately: 'I'm not sure that I would stop.'*

---

* I often strike a balance between a strong desire and an accident of which I am either the instigator or the victim,

Once I had dressed, made up, done my hair and tidied the house, if I still had some time left, I would be incapable of reading or marking essays. In a way, too, I didn't want my mind to concentrate on anything else but the wait itself, in order not to spoil it. Quite often I would write down on a sheet of paper the date, the time and 'he's going to come', along with other sentences, fears – that he might not come, that he might not feel the same desire for me. In the evening I would go back to the sheet of paper, 'he came', jotting down the details of that meeting at random. Then, dazed, I would stare at the scrawls on the paper and the two paragraphs written before and after, which one read in succession without a break. In between there had been words and gestures which made everything else seem trivial, including the very

an illness, or some other tragedy. Knowing whether I would agree to pay the imaginary price of disaster is a sure means of assessing the strength of my desire, possibly also of challenging fate: 'I don't care if the house burns down so long as I manage to finish writing this book.'

writing destined to capture them. An interval of time squeezed in between two car noises – his Renault 25 braking, then driving off again – when I knew that nothing in my life (having children, passing exams, travelling to faraway countries) had ever meant as much to me as lying in bed with that man in the middle of the afternoon.

It would only last for a few hours. I never wore my watch, removing it just before he arrived. He would keep his on and I dreaded the moment when he would glance at it discreetly. When I went into the kitchen to get some ice, I would look up at the clock hanging above the door: 'only two more hours', 'only one more hour' or 'in one hour I'll be here and he'll be gone'. Astonished, I asked myself: 'Where is the present?'

He would dress slowly before leaving. I would watch him button up his shirt, put on his socks, his underpants, his trousers, then turn towards the mirror to fasten his tie. After he had put on his jacket, it would all be over. Now I was only time flowing through myself.

As soon as he left, I would be overcome by a wave of fatigue. I wouldn't tidy up straight away: I would sit staring at the glasses, the plates and their leftovers, the overflowing ashtray, the clothes, the lingerie strewn all over the bedroom and the hallway, the sheets spilling over on to the carpet. I would have liked to keep that mess the way it was – a mess in which every object evoked a caress or a particular moment, forming a still-life whose intensity and pain could never, for me, be captured by any painting in a museum. Naturally I would never wash until the next day, to keep his sperm inside me.

I would count the number of times we had made love. I felt that each time something new had been added to our relationship but that somehow this very accumulation of touching and pleasure would eventually draw us apart. We were burning up a capital of desire. What we gained in physical intensity we lost in time.

[10]

I would slip into a semi-slumber which gave me the sensation I was sleeping in his body. The following day I would enter a state of apathy, forever reliving a caress he had given me or repeating a word he had spoken. He didn't know any coarse words in French or maybe he chose not to use them because they were not suggestive of social taboo; they were innocent words, just like the others. (The same would have applied to me in the case of obscene words belonging to his language.) In the subway, at the supermarket, I would hear his voice whisper to me: 'Stroke my penis with your mouth.' Once, lost in a daydream on the platform at the Opera subway station, I let my train go by without even realizing it.

This lethargic condition would gradually ease and I would start expecting his phone call again, with all the more suffering and anxiety as the date of our last meeting receded. As in the past, when the longer I waited after taking an exam the more I became convinced I had failed, so now, as the days went by without him ringing, I was certain he had left me.

In his absence, I was only happy when I was out buying new dresses, earrings, stockings, and trying them on at home in front of the mirror—the ideal, quite impossible, being that he should see me each time in a different outfit. He would only glimpse my new blouse or pumps for a couple of minutes before they were discarded in some corner until he left. Of course I realized how pointless new clothes were in the event of his feeling desire for another woman. But presenting myself in clothes he had already seen seemed a mistake, a slackening in the quest for perfection for which I strove in my relationship with him. In the same spirit of perfection, I once browsed through *Techniques of Lovemaking* in a supermarket. Beneath the title one could read: '700,000 copies sold'.

Quite often I felt I was living out this passion in

the same way I would have written a book: the same determination to get every single scene right, the same minute attention to detail. I could even accept the thought of dying providing I had lived this passion through to the very end – without actually defining 'to the very end' – in the same way I could die in a few months' time after finishing this book.

In front of people I knew, I tried not to betray my obsession by words, although to exercise such self-control continually is extremely taxing. At the hairdresser's one day I saw a talkative woman to whom everyone had been speaking perfectly normally until she announced, her head tilted back over the basin: 'I'm being treated for my nerves.' Immediately, the staff stiffened and addressed her with distant reserve, as if this irrepressible confession were proof of her insanity. I feared I would also be considered abnormal if I had said: 'I'm having a passionate love affair.' Yet when I was among other women, at the supermarket check-out or at the bank, I wondered whether they too were wrapped up in a man. If they weren't, how could they go on living this way – that is to say, judging by my previous standards, with nothing else to wait for but the weekend, a meal out, the gym class or the children's school results: things for which I now felt aversion or indifference.

When someone confided in me, a man or a woman who admitted they were having, or had had, 'a crazy love affair with a guy' or 'a very close relationship with someone', I occasionally felt like opening up. But once the excitement of sharing our secrets was over, I resented having let myself go, if only a little. Those conversations, when I had continually responded to the other person by saying 'me too, it's the same for me, I did that too', suddenly seemed futile, removed from the reality of my own passion. Rather, something was lost through these outbursts.

To my sons – students who come and stay with me once in a while – I had revealed only the barest practicalities that enabled me to conduct my liaison satisfactorily. They had to call me to find out whether they could come and stay and, if they were already at home, agree to leave as soon as A announced his visit. These arrangements – so it seemed – did not cause any problems. However I would have preferred to have kept my children completely out of this, in the same way I had never mentioned boyfriends or lovers to my parents in the past. Probably because I feared their judgement. Also, parents and children are the last people able to accept freely the sexuality of those who are closest to them and so remain forever inaccessible. Children will always refuse to see the truth reflected in their mother's absent stare and silent behavior: at times they mean nothing to her, in the same way that grown-up kittens can mean nothing to a mother cat longing to go on the prowl.★

★ A panel of young people interviewed by the women's magazine *Marie-Claire* strongly condemned the love affairs of their mothers, either divorced or living on their own. One girl remarked bitterly: 'All my mother's lovers could do was to help her escape into her dreams.' Who could ask for more?

Throughout this period, I didn't once listen to any classical music; I preferred songs. Sentimental songs, which previously I had ignored, moved me deeply. In a simple, straightforward manner, they spoke of the absolute, universal nature of passion. When I heard Sylvie Vartan sing, *'c'est fatal, animal'*, I knew I wasn't the only woman to feel that way. Songs accompanied and legitimized my own experience.

In women's magazines I would always start by reading the horoscope.

I would feel the sudden urge to go and see such and such a film, convinced that it encapsulated my own story, bitterly

[17]

disappointed if, as in the case of an early film like Oshima's *Empire of the Senses*, it was no longer showing anywhere.

I would give money to the men and women sitting in the corridors of the Metro, making the wish that he would call me that evening. I promised to send two hundred francs to UNICEF if he came to see me before a particular date I had chosen. Breaking with my usual lifestyle, I was inclined to be spendthrift. I felt that wasting money was part of an over-all investment, necessary and inseparable from my passion for A; it also included the time spent on waiting and daydreaming and, naturally, the time spent on my body: making love until I dropped with exhaustion, as if it were for the last time. (And who can say that it isn't for the last time?)

One afternoon when he was there, I burned the living-room carpet down to the weft by placing a boiling coffee pot on top of it. I didn't care. Quite the contrary. I was happy every time I caught sight of the mark as I remembered that afternoon with him.

I was unaffected by the inconveniences of daily life. I didn't worry about a two-month postal strike since A never wrote to me (no doubt the cautious attitude of a married man). I would sit calmly through traffic jams and queue patiently at the bank, and was not annoyed by the surly attitude of a clerk. Nothing could make me lose my temper. I felt pain, sympathy and compassion for other people. I understood the dropouts lying on benches, the clients of prostitutes or a passenger engrossed in her Harlequin romance (although I was incapable of saying why I resembled them).

One day, as I was going naked to the refrigerator to get some beer, I remembered the women, single or married, mothers with children, living in my old neighbourhood, who secretly received a man in the afternoon. (Rumor was rife: it was impossible to say whether people reproached them for their improper conduct or for the fact that they devoted the daylight hours to lovemaking instead of cleaning the windows.) I thought of these women with acute satisfaction.

During all this time, I felt I was living out my passion in the manner of a novel but now I'm not sure in which style I am writing about it: in the style of a testimony, possibly even the sort of confidence one finds in women's magazines, a manifesto or a statement, or maybe a critical commentary.

I am not giving the account of a liaison, I am not telling a story (half of which escapes me) based on a precise – he came on 11 November – or an approximate chronology – weeks went by. As far as I was concerned, that notion did not enter the relationship; I could experience only absence or presence. I am merely listing the signs of a passion, wavering between 'one day' and 'every day', as if this inventory could allow me to grasp the reality of my passion. Naturally, in the listing and description of these facts, there is no irony or derision, which are ways of telling things to people or to oneself after the event, and not experiencing them at the time.

As for the origins of my passion, I have no intention of searching for them in my early history – which one reconstitutes with the help of a psychoanalyst – or in my recent history, or for that matter in the cultural standards governing emotion which have influenced me since childhood (*Gone with the Wind*, *Phèdre* or the songs of Edith Piaf are just as decisive as the Oedipus complex). I do not wish to explain my passion – that would imply that it was a mistake or some disorder I need to justify – I just want to describe it.

Maybe the only criteria to be taken into account should be of a material order: the time and freedom available to me throughout the affair.

He liked Yves Saint-Laurent suits, Cerruti ties and powerful cars. He drove fast, flashing his headlights, without a word, as if carried away by the exhilaration of being free, well-dressed and in a position of authority on a French motorway, he who came from Eastern Europe. He liked being told that he resembled Alain Delon. I suspected – as far as one reasonably can in the case of a foreigner – that although he respected them, he was not drawn to artistic or intellectual matters. When it came to television, he preferred the quizzes and *Santa Barbara*. I didn't mind in the least. No doubt because I attributed A's tastes – those of a foreigner – above all to cultural differences, whereas in the case of a Frenchman, they would have been seen by me as social differences. Maybe, too, it was because I liked to recognize in A the 'parvenu' part of myself: as a teenager I would crave dresses, records and trips abroad, deprived of these things among friends who had them – just like A himself, 'deprived' along with the whole of his country, longing to possess the expensive shirts and video recorders displayed in Western shops.*

He was a heavy drinker, as people often are in Eastern European countries. It worried me because of the possibility of an accident when he drove back on the motorway, but I wasn't disgusted. Even if he occasionally stumbled, or belched when kissing me. On the contrary, I was happy to be close to him in these moments of incipient abjection.

I wasn't quite sure how to qualify his

---

* This man continues to live somewhere in the world. I cannot describe him in greater detail, or supply information that might lead to his identification. He has 'built his life' with determination; in other words, nothing is more important for him than to work towards building this life. The fact that I have different priorities does not give me the right to reveal his identity. He did not choose to play a part in this book, only in my life.

[23]

relationship with me. In the beginning I had deduced from certain signs that he experienced the same passion as me – his radiant expression and his silence when he looked at me, saying 'I drove like a madman to get here', telling me about his childhood. This certainty gradually wavered. He seemed to be more distant, less inclined to open up, but he only had to talk about his father, or the raspberries he went picking in the woods at the age of twelve, for me to change my mind. He stopped giving me presents. When I received flowers or a book from friends, I thought of the attentions he no longer lavished on me. Then immediately: 'He gives me his desire.' I would drink in the sentences which I thought betrayed his jealousy, the only proof of his love in my eyes. After a while I realized that 'are you going away for Christmas?' was no more than a simple, practical question, to decide whether or not to fix a meeting, and certainly not a roundabout way of finding out if I was going skiing with someone else (maybe he even wanted me to leave so that he could see another woman). I often wondered what these afternoons of lovemaking meant to him. Probably nothing more than just that, making love. There was no point looking for other reasons. I would only ever be certain of one thing: his desire or lack of desire. The only undeniable truth could be glimpsed by looking at his penis.

The fact that he was a foreigner made it all the more difficult to understand his behavior, molded by a culture which I knew only through folklore and clichés for tourists. At first I was discouraged by the obvious limitations of our exchanges. These were emphasized by the fact that, although he spoke fairly good French, I could not express myself in his language. Later I realized that this situation spared me the illusion that we shared a perfect relationship, or even formed a whole. Because his French strayed slightly from standard use and because I occasionally had doubts about the meaning he gave to words, I was able to appreciate the approximate quality of our conversations. From the very beginning, and throughout the whole of our affair, I had the privilege of knowing what we all find out in the end: the man we love is a complete stranger.

The constraints dictated by his married condition – not being able to phone him or send him letters, not giving him presents which would prove difficult to justify, being continually dependent on his timetable – did not outrage me. I would give him the letters I had written to him when he was leaving the house. I suspected that once he had read them he probably tore them up on the motorway but this didn't stop me writing. I was careful not to leave evidence of myself on his clothes and made no marks on his body. Naturally, I wanted to spare him a scene with his wife but I also feared arousing resentment on his behalf, which might have led him to stop seeing me. For precisely this reason, I avoided meeting him in places where she accompanied him. I was afraid that in front of her I would betray the bond between us by a familiar gesture –

stroking the nape of A's neck, adjusting his clothes and so on. (Also, I didn't want to suffer unnecessarily by imagining A making love to her, which happened every time I saw her. The fact that I considered her to be plain, or that he did it simply because he had her 'close at hand' did nothing to lessen the torment of this vision.)

Strangely enough, these very constraints bred waiting and desire. As he always called me from telephone booths, whose functioning could prove erratic, quite often when I picked up the receiver there was no one on the line. After some time I realized that this 'fake' phone call would be followed by the real one, fifteen minutes later at the most, the time it took to find a phone booth in working order. That first silent call was a prelude to his voice, a (rare) promise of happiness, and the interval separating it from the second call – when he would say my name and 'can we meet?' – one of the most glorious moments ever.

In front of my television set in the evening, I

[27]

wondered if he was watching the same program or film, especially if the subject was love or sex, or if the script bore a resemblance to our situation. I imagined he was watching *La femme d'à côté*, substituting us for the characters in the movie. If he told me that he had indeed seen the film, I was inclined to believe that he had chosen it that evening because of us and that, acted out on the screen, our story must have seemed more intense, or at least more legitimate. (Naturally, I soon dismissed the idea that our liaison might appear dangerous to him – in films, any passion existing outside marriage invariably ends in disaster.)*

Sometimes I told myself that he might spend a whole day without even thinking about me. I imagined him getting up, drinking his coffee, talking and laughing, as if I didn't exist. Compared to my own obsession, such indifference filled me with wonder. How could this be. He himself would have been astonished

* Maurice Pialat's *Loulou*, Bertrand Blier's *Trop belle pour toi*, for example.

[28]

to find out that I never stopped thinking about him from morning to night. There was nothing to suggest that my attitude was more justifiable than his. In a way, I was luckier than him.

Walking around Paris, when I saw large cars zooming along the avenues, driven by men on their own resembling high-powered executives, I realized that A was no different from these men, concerned primarily with his career, with bouts of eroticism, possibly love, for a new woman every two or three years. This discovery came as a release. I would decide to stop seeing him. I was certain that he had become as anonymous and insignificant as those yuppies in their BMWs and Renault 25s. But while I was walking, I would look at the dresses and the lingerie in the shop windows, as if anticipating our next meeting.

These fleeting moments of detachment were prompted by external factors; I did not wish for them. On the contrary, I avoided every opportunity that might tear me away from my obsession – books, social engagements and the other activities I used to enjoy. I longed for total idleness. I angrily turned down some extra work my boss had asked me to do, almost insulting him over the phone. I felt I had every right to reject the things that prevented me from luxuriating in the sensations and fantasies of my own passion.

On railway platforms, in the Metro, in waiting rooms, places where you are allowed to do nothing at all, as soon as I sat down, I would start daydreaming about A. A shudder of happiness would course through me the very second I entered that state. I felt I was giving in to physical pleasure, as if the brain, exposed to a repeated flow of the same images and memories, could achieve an orgasm, becoming a sexual organ like the others.

Naturally I feel no shame in writing these things because of the time which separates the moment when they are written – when only I can see them – from the moment when they will be read by other people, a moment which I feel will never come. By then I could have had an accident or died; a war or a revolution could have broken out. This delay makes it possible for me to write today, in the same way I used to lie in the scorching sun for a whole day at sixteen, or make love without contraceptives at twenty: without thinking about the consequences.

(It is a mistake therefore to compare someone writing about his own life to an exhibitionist, since the latter has only one desire: to show himself and to be seen at the same time.)

In the spring my waiting became continual. An early heatwave had set in since the first days of May. Summer dresses appeared on the streets; café terraces were crowded. All over town one heard the strains of an exotic dance, murmured by a woman with a rasping voice, the *Lambada*. Everything conspired to evoke new forms of pleasure which I was sure A planned to enjoy outside my company. His position and professional responsibilities in France seemed important to me, and likely to arouse the admiration of all women. Conversely, I would belittle myself, failing to find any reason that might hold him back. Whenever I went to Paris, I would expect to see him drive past with a woman by his side. I would walk very straight, affecting an attitude of proud indifference in anticipation of our meeting. The fact that this meeting, understandably, never took place, succeeded only in frustrating me: I would stride down the Boulevard des Italiens, bathed in sweat, under his imaginary gaze while he was in fact somewhere else, inaccessible. The sight of him driving towards the park in Sceaux or the wood in Vincennes, with the windows down and the radio at full volume, haunted me.

One day, in a television weekly, I began reading about a troupe of Cuban dancers who were on tour in Paris. The author of the article stressed the sensuality and permissiveness of Cuban women. A photograph showed the dancer who had been interviewed, tall, with dark hair, her long legs exposed. As I read on, my intuition grew stronger and stronger. By the time I had finished the article, I was convinced that A, who had been to Cuba, had met the girl in the photograph. I imagined them together in a hotel room and nothing at that point could have persuaded me that this scene was improbable. On the contrary, the very idea that it had not taken place seemed to me absurd, inconceivable.

When he rang to arrange a meeting, his long-awaited call had no effect on me and I remained locked in the same state of anxiety as before. My condition was such that not even the sound of his voice could make me happy. It was all infinite emptiness, except when we were together making love. And even then I dreaded the moments to come, when he would be gone. I experienced pleasure like a future pain.

I longed to end the affair, so as not to be at the mercy of a phone call, so as not to suffer, realizing at once what this would entail, seconds after the separation: a series of days with nothing to wait for. I preferred to carry on at any cost – let him have another woman, or even several. (In other words, accepting a torment far greater than the one which made me want to leave him.) Compared to such emptiness, my present situation seemed enviable and my jealousy a sort of frail privilege which I would have been mad to want to end since one day it would end anyway, outside my control, when he would leave the country or would decide to stop seeing me.

I avoided opportunities of meeting him in public, in the company of other people, as I couldn't bear the thought of seeing him just for the sake of it. Therefore I didn't go to an inauguration to which he had been invited, obsessed by his image throughout the evening: smiling, showering a woman with attentions, the same way he had behaved with me when we first met. Afterwards I was told that only a handful of people had turned up. I was relieved and took pleasure in repeating the expression, as if there existed a link between the atmosphere of a party, the number of women invited, and what could only be dictated by chance circumstances, in other words, his desire or not to flirt, in which case a single woman was enough.

I tried to find out what he did in his spare time and where he went away for the weekend. I would say to myself, 'right now he's in Fontainebleau forest, he's out running', 'he's driving towards Deauville', 'he's sitting on the beach next to his wife' and so on. This knowledge comforted me. I felt that if I could locate him in a particular place at a particular time, I would be immune to an infidelity on his part. (A similar belief, equally deep-rooted, leads me to believe that knowing where my sons are – at a party or on holiday – is enough to save them from an accident, drugs or drowning.)

I didn't want to go away on holiday that summer and wake up in the morning with the prospect of having to spend a whole day without waiting for his phone call. But giving up my holiday would have meant spelling out my passion to him more eloquently than by saying, 'I am crazy about you.' One day, seized by the desire to break up, I decided instead to book a train ticket and a hotel room in Florence for a date two months ahead. This type of separation suited me perfectly as it meant I didn't have to leave him. I anticipated the moment of my departure the way I would have anticipated an exam for which I had enrolled long in advance and failed to study: with despondency and a feeling of hopelessness. Lying on my bunk in the sleeping car, I kept seeing myself in that same train, this time heading back towards Paris, eight days later: the promise of supreme happiness, almost too good to be true (I might die in Florence, I might never see him again), increased my horror at moving further and further away from Paris, turning the interval of time between the two train journeys into an unbearable, interminable wait.

The worst part was not being able to stay in my room all day, waiting for the train that would take me back to Paris. I had to justify my trip by visiting places of cultural interest and by going for walks, which I often do on holiday. I walked for hours, in the Oltrarno, the Boboli Gardens, up to the Piazza San

Michelangelo and San Miniato. I went into each of the churches that was open and made three wishes, sustained by the belief that one of the three would come true (naturally, all three were related to A). There, I sat in the cool and the silence, indulging in one of the many scenarios which occurred to me continually, wherever I was, from morning to night (a trip together to Florence, meeting him at an airport ten years later and so on).

I couldn't understand why people looked up the date and the history of each painting in their guidebook. Such things had nothing to do with their own lives. My approach to works of art was purely emotional. I went back to La Badia because it was there that Dante had met Beatrice. The partly-erased frescoes in Santa Croce moved me because of my story, which would come to resemble them one day – fading fragments in his memory and in mine.

In museums I saw only the works representing love. I was drawn to statues of naked men. In them I recognized the shape of A's shoulders, his loïns, his penis, and especially the slight hollow following the inner curve of the thigh up to the groin. I was unable to tear myself away from Michelangelo's *David*, filled with wonder that a man, and not a woman, had portrayed the beauty of a male body so sublimely. Even if this could be explained by the oppressed condition of women, it seemed to me that something had been irretrievably lost.*

On the train, on the way back, I felt that I had literally written out my passion in Florence by walking through the streets, visiting the museums, obsessed by A, sharing everything with him, eating and sleeping with him in that noisy hotel on the banks of the River Arno. I need only go back to read this story of a woman in love with a man, which was my story. Those eight days on my own, without speaking, except to waiters in restaurants,

---

* Similarly, I regretted that no woman had ever produced a painting as indescribably moving as that by Courbet, exposing the open thighs of a recumbent woman, her face invisible, entitled *The Origins of the World*.

haunted by the image of A – I was astonished to be accosted by men, could they not see him silhouetted inside my own body? – were seen by me as an ordeal for the betterment of love. A sort of further investment, this time in imagination and craving through absence.

He left France and went back to his own country six months ago. I shall probably never see him again. At first, when I woke up at two o'clock in the morning, I didn't care whether I lived or died. My whole body ached. I would have liked to tear out the pain but it was everywhere. I longed for a burglar to come into my bedroom and kill me. During the day I tried desperately to find things to do, so as not to remain idle, otherwise I felt I would be lost (the meaning of the word was vague: to have a nervous breakdown, to start drinking, and so on). For the same reason, I made efforts to dress and put on makeup properly, and to wear my contact lenses instead of my spectacles, although this required considerable courage. I couldn't watch television or leaf through magazines; all the advertisements, whether they are for perfume or microwaves, show the same thing: a woman waiting for a man. I averted my gaze when I walked past shops selling lingerie.

When I was feeling really bad, I had a strong urge to consult a fortune-teller; it seemed the only decisive thing I could do. One day I looked up the names of clairvoyants in the electronic directory. The list was long. One of them mentioned that she had predicted the earthquake in San Francisco and the death of the singer Dalida. While I was jotting down their names and phone numbers, I felt the same excitement as the month before, when I was trying on a new dress for A, as if I were still doing something for him. I didn't call any of the fortune-tellers; I was afraid they would predict he would never return. I thought to myself with surprise, 'I've come round to this too.' After all, there was no reason why I shouldn't have.

One night the thought of getting myself screened for AIDS occurred to me: 'At least he would have left me that.'

I wanted to remember his body with all my being – from his hair down to the tips of his toes. I could conjure up, vividly, his green eyes, the lock of hair falling over his forehead, the curve of his shoulders. I could feel his teeth, the inside of his mouth, the shape of his thighs, the texture of his skin. I reflected that there was very little difference between this reconstruction and an hallucination, between memory and madness.

One day, lying on my stomach, I gave myself an orgasm; somehow I felt that it was his orgasm.

For many weeks:
> I would wake up in the middle of the night, and remain in a confused state until morning, awake, incapable of thinking. I wanted to lose myself in a deep sleep but he continued to hover above me.

I didn't want to get up. I would see the day stretch ahead of me, with no plans. I felt that time was no longer taking me anywhere, it only made me grow old.

At the supermarket I would say to myself, 'I don't need to buy that any more' (whisky, salted almonds and so on).

I would look at the blouses and the pairs of shoes I had bought to please a man, now meaningless clothes, existing solely for the sake of fashion. Was it possible to long for these things, or for anything else, other than in connection with a man, other than to serve the cause of love? I had to buy a shawl because of the bitter cold: 'He will never see it.'

I could no longer stand the company of others. The only people I saw were those I had met during my relationship with A. They featured in my passion. Even if they failed to arouse my interest or sympathy, somehow I was fond of them. But I could not watch a television presenter, an actor whose eyes, appearance and comic expressions used to remind me of A. These signs of him in a person I didn't care about were something of an imposture. I hated these men for continuing to look like A.

I would make wishes: if he calls me before the end of the month, I'll give five hundred francs to a charity. I imagined that we had met in a hotel, at an airport, or that he had sent me a letter. I replied to words he had never spoken, sentences he would never write.

If I went to the same place I had been to last year, when he was here, I would wear the same suit as before, trying to convince myself that identical circumstances produce identical effects and that he would call me that evening. When I went to bed around midnight, thoroughly demoralized, I realized that I had really believed in that phone call all day.

During my spells of insomnia, I would take myself back to Venice, where I had spent a week's holiday just before meeting A. I tried to recall my timetable and the places I had visited; I imagined myself walking along the Zattere and the alleys of Giudecca Island. I would reconstitute my room in the annexe of La Calcina Hotel, straining to remember every detail: the narrow bed, the blocked window giving on to the back of the Café Cucciolo, the table and its cloth on which I had placed some books. I would reel off the titles of the books. I would enumerate the things that were there, one after the other, attempting to chronicle the contents of a place where I had stayed before my story with A had started, as if an exhaustive inventory would enable me to relive the events. Driven by the same belief, I sometimes felt the urge actually to return to Venice, to the same hotel, the same room.

Throughout this period, all my thoughts and all my actions involved the repetition of history. I wanted to turn the present back into the past, opening on to happiness.

I was always calculating, 'it's two weeks, five weeks since he left' or 'last year, around this time, I was there, I was doing that'. Whatever the occasion – the opening of a shopping mall,

Gorbachev's visit to Paris, Chang's victory at Roland-Garros – I immediately thought: 'That was when he was here.' I would relive moments of that period, insignificant in themselves – I am standing in the archive room at La Sorbonne, I am walking along Boulevard Voltaire, I am trying on a skirt in a Benetton shop – with such vivid detail that I wondered why it wasn't possible to *slip into* that particular day or moment as easily as one slips into another room.

In my dreams too was the desire to reverse time. I spoke and argued with my deceased mother, alive once more, although in my dream both of us knew that she was dead. There was nothing extraordinary about this, her death was behind her now; somehow it was 'out of the way'. (I believe this dream recurred several times.) On another occasion, it was about a little girl in a swimsuit who had disappeared during an outing. The reconstruction of the murder took place immediately afterwards. The child revived to retrace the events that had led to her death. For the judge, however, knowing the truth made the reconstruction even more complicated. In the other dreams, I lost my way, mislaid my handbag, found myself unable to pack my suitcase in time to catch a train leaving minutes later. I caught sight of A, surrounded by other people. He wasn't looking at me. We were together in a taxi; I was stroking him, his penis remained limp. Later, he appeared again in front of me with his desire evident. We met in the lavatory of a café, in the street, by a wall. He took me without a word.

On weekends I would make myself do heavy physical work, gardening or cleaning the house. In the evening I was exhausted, my limbs aching, as they had been when A had spent the afternoon at my place. But in this case the fatigue I experienced was hollow, without the memory of another body, and it repelled me.

I began writing, 'From September last year, I did nothing else but wait for a man . . .', approximately two months after A's departure; I don't remember the exact day. Although I can clearly recall everything that happened during my relationship with A – the October riots in Algeria, the heat and the hazy sky on 14 July 1989, even the most trivial details such as the acquisition of a blender in June the day before we were due to meet – I find it quite impossible to associate the writing of a particular page with a rainstorm or any one of the events that have occurred in the world over the past five months: the fall of the Berlin wall or the execution of the Ceauşescus. Living in passion or writing: in each case one's perception of time is fundamentally different.

Yet, when I began to write, I wanted to stay in that age of passion, when all my actions – from the choice of a film to the selection of a lipstick – were channelled toward one person. The past tense used in the first part of the book suggests endless repetition and conveys the belief that 'life was better in those days'. It also generated a pain that was to replace the

[49]

past trauma of waiting for his phone calls and visits. (Even now, rereading those first pages has the same distressing effect as seeing and touching the terry-cloth bathrobe he used to slip on at my place, and take off just before he got dressed to leave. There is one difference, though: these pages will always mean something to me, to others too maybe, whereas the bathrobe – which matters only to me – will lose all significance one day and will be added to a bundle of rags. By writing this, I may also be wanting to save the bathrobe from oblivion.)

Yet I went on living. In other words, the act of writing didn't lessen my grief. As soon as I had set down my pen, I felt pangs for the man whose voice and foreign accent I could no longer hear, whose skin I could no longer touch, living an unknown life in some cold city – the real man, far more inaccessible than the written man designated by the letter A. And so I went on doing the things that help alleviate sorrow, offering hope when, theoretically, there is no longer cause for any:

playing patience, slipping a ten-franc coin into a beggar's paper cup at Auber Metro station, making the wish that 'he'll call, he'll come back'. (Perhaps, after all, writing is one of these things.)

Despite my aversion to meeting people, I agreed to attend a seminar in Copenhagen because it was an opportunity to send him news of me discreetly: a postcard I felt he would have to answer. As soon as I arrived in Copenhagen, I thought of nothing else: buying a card, copying out the few sentences I had carefully written before leaving, finding a letter box. On the plane, on the way back, I reflected that I had travelled to Denmark simply to send a postcard to a man.

I felt like rereading one or the other of the books I had skimmed through when A. was there. I felt that the waiting and the dreams of that period had crystallized within the pages and that I would rediscover my passion, intact. Yet I was reluctant to do so, postponing the moment when I would open the first page, almost out of superstition, as if *Anna Karenina* were some esoteric work in which it would be forbidden to turn a particular page on pain of ill-fortune.

One day I felt an overriding urge to go to the Passage Cardinet, in the 17th *arrondissement*, to the place where I had a clandestine abortion twenty years ago. I felt it was imperative that I return to see the street, the building, and go up to the flat where the events had taken place. Vaguely hoping that this past trauma would cancel my present grief.

I got out at Malesherbes Metro station, on a square whose name, recently changed, meant nothing to me. I had to stop at a grocer's shop to ask the way. The lettering on the plaque bearing the name of the Passage Cardinet is partly erased. The façades are newly restored, white. I went to the street number I remembered and pushed open the door, one of the few remaining ones not to be protected by a digital code. On the wall hung the list of tenants. The old woman, an auxiliary nurse, had died or been moved to an old people's home in the suburbs; the residents living in the street now belong to the high income bracket. As I was heading towards Pont-Cardinet, I saw myself walking beside the old woman, who had insisted on accompanying me to the nearest station, no doubt to make sure that I wouldn't collapse on her doorstep with a tube up my belly. I thought: 'I was here one day.' I wondered what the difference was between this past reality and literature, perhaps just a feeling of disbelief that I had actually been there one day, something I wouldn't have felt in the case of a fictional character.

I went back to Malesherbes station and took the Metro. This episode had altered nothing, yet I was glad to have taken the initiative and revived an act of despoilment, also caused by a man.

(Am I the only woman to return to the scene of an abortion? Sometimes I wonder if the purpose of my writing is to find out whether other people have done or felt the same things or, if not, for them to consider experiencing such things as normal. Maybe I would also like them to live out these very emotions in turn, forgetting that they had once read about them somewhere.)

Now it's April. Sometimes I wake up in the morning without immediately thinking of A. The prospect of rediscovering 'life's little pleasures' – meeting friends, going to the cinema, enjoying a good meal – has become less horrific. I am still in the age of passion (one day I will no longer be aware that I wasn't thinking of A when I woke up) but it has changed, it has ceased to be continuous.*

* For want of a better solution, I have switched from the past to the present, although it is impossible to establish the demarcation line between the two tenses. I am incapable of describing the way in which my passion for A developed day by day. I can only freeze certain moments in time and single out isolated symptoms of a phenomenon whose chronology remains uncertain – as in the case of historical events.

Suddenly I remember details about him, things he said to me. For instance, that he had gone to the Moscow Circus and that the cat trainer was 'incredible'. For a brief moment I feel supremely calm, as I am when I emerge from a dream in which I have seen him, but don't yet know that I was dreaming. The feeling that everything is back to normal and that 'now it's all right'. Then I realize that these words refer to some remote past: another winter has gone by, the cat trainer may have left the circus, the expression 'he's incredible' belongs to a reality which is long outdated.

In the course of conversation, I occasionally glimpse one of A's attitudes or discover an aspect of our relationship that had previously escaped me. A colleague with whom I was having coffee once told me that he'd had an extremely physical relationship with a married woman older than himself: 'On leaving her place, I would brace myself and sniff the evening air, swept by a glorious feeling of masculinity.' It occurred to me that A may have experienced the same sensation. I was pleased by this discovery, although it was

[55]

impossible to check, as if I had captured something imperishable that cannot be conveyed by memories.

In the Metro tonight, two girls sitting opposite me were chatting. I heard one of them say, 'They've got a house in Barbizon.' I wondered why the name was familiar and, after a few minutes, remembered that A had told me he had spent one Sunday there with his wife. It was a memory like any other, that, for instance, suggested by the name Brunoy, where an old friend I had lost touch with was living. So the world is beginning to mean something again outside A? The cat trainer from the Moscow Circus, the towelling bathrobe, Barbizon, the entire text assembled in my head day after day since the first night with words, images and gestures, all the signs forming the unwritten novel of a passion are beginning to fall apart. Of the living text, this book is only the remainder, a minor trace. One day it will mean nothing to me, just like its living counterpart.

Yet I cannot resolve to part with it, just as I was unable to leave A last spring, when my waiting and desire for him were continual. I know full well that I can expect nothing from writing, which, unlike real life, rules out the unexpected. To go on writing is also a means of delaying the trauma of giving this to others to read. I hadn't considered this eventuality while I still felt the need to write. But now that I have satisfied this need, I stare at the written pages with astonishment and something resembling shame, feelings I certainly never felt when I was living out my passion and writing about it. The prospect of publication brings me closer to people's judgement and the 'normal' values of society. (Having to answer questions such as 'Is it an autobiography?' and having to justify this or that may have stopped many books from seeing the light of day, except in the form of a novel, which succeeds in saving appearances.)

At this point, sitting in front of the pages covered in my indecipherable scrawlings, which only I can interpret, I can still believe this is something private, almost childish, of no consequence whatsoever – like the declarations of love and the obscene expressions I used to write on the back of my exercise books in class, or anything else one may write calmly, in all impunity, when there is no risk of it being read. Once I start typing out the text, once it appears before me in public characters, I shall be through with innocence.

February 1991

I could end the book here and pretend that nothing that goes on in the world or in my life could affect this text. In other words, I could consider it removed from time and ready for publication. However, so long as these pages remain personal and within my reach, as they are today, the act of writing will be open. I feel it is more important to mention certain recent developments than to alter the position of an adjective.

Between last May, when I stopped writing, and today, 6 February 1991, the expected conflict between Iraq and the Western coalition has finally broken out. A 'clean' war according to the propagandists, although Iraq has already received 'more bombs than the whole of Germany during the Second World War' (this evening's edition of *Le Monde*) and eyewitnesses claim to have seen children stumbling through the streets of Baghdad like drunkards, deafened by the explosions. Here we can only wait for disasters which have been forecast but do not in fact happen: a land offensive led by the 'Allies', a chemical warfare attack by Saddam Hussein, a bomb outrage perhaps at the Galeries Lafayette department store. I experience the same feeling of anxiety, the same frustrated desire to know the truth as I did when I was living out my passion. The resemblance ends there. For in this case there is no room for fantasy or imagination.

On the first Sunday of the war, in the evening, the phone rang. A's voice. For a split second, I was seized with panic. I kept repeating his name, crying. He said, 'It's me, it's me', slowly. He wanted to see me now, at once; he would take a taxi. In the half-hour I had left before he arrived, I dressed and made up in a frenzy. Then I waited in the hallway, wrapped in the shawl he had never seen. I stared at the door in disbelief. He came in without knocking, the way he used to. He must have been drinking; he was swaying when he embraced me and he stumbled on his way upstairs to the bedroom.

Afterwards, all he wanted was coffee. It seems that his life in the East is no different: the same job as in France, and still no child, although his wife would like to have one. At thirty-eight he still has a youthful appearance although now he looks wearier. His nails are less tidy, his hands less smooth, probably because of the cold climate in his country. He was greatly amused when I told him off for not having kept in touch since he left: 'So I would have called you up; hello, how are things? And then what?' He hadn't received the postcard I sent him from Denmark, addressed to his former workplace in Paris. We dressed again, picking up our clothes tangled on the tiled floor, and I drove him back to his hotel near the Etoile. We kissed and touched each other at the traffic lights between Nanterre and Pont-de-Neuilly.

In the tunnel at La Défense, on my way back, I thought, 'Where is my story?' Then, 'Now I can hope for nothing more.'

He left three days later without us meeting

again. Before leaving, over the phone, he said, 'I'll call you.' I don't know if this means he will call me from his country, or from Paris, when he gets an opportunity to come back. I didn't ask him.

I have the impression that this last visit never took place. It doesn't belong to our story, it's just a date, 20 January. The man who returned that evening wasn't the man I was carrying inside me throughout the year when he was here, and when I was writing about him. I shall never see that man again. Yet it is that surreal, almost non-existent last visit that gives my passion its true meaning, which is precisely to be meaningless, and to have been for two years the most violent and unaccountable reality ever.

On this photograph, the only one I have of him, I can see a tall, fair man, bearing a slight resemblance to Alain Delon. Everything about him was precious to me – his eyes, his mouth, his penis, his childhood memories, his voice and the decisive way he took hold of things.

I had decided to learn his language. I kept, without washing it, a glass from which he had drunk.

I had wished that the plane flying back from Copenhagen would crash if I were never to see him again.

Last summer in Padua I pressed this photograph to the wall of St Anthony's tomb – along with people pressing a handkerchief or a folded slip of paper bearing their prayers – so that he would come back.

Whether or not he was 'worth it' is of no consequence. And the fact that all this is gradually slipping away from me, as if it concerned another woman, does not change this one truth: thanks to him, I was able to approach the frontier separating me from others, to the extent of actually believing that I could sometimes cross over it.

I measured time differently, with all my body.

I discovered what people are capable of,

in other words, anything: sublime or deadly desires, lack of dignity, attitudes and beliefs I had found absurd in others until I myself turned to them. Without knowing it, he brought me closer to the world.

He had said, 'You won't write a book about me.' But I haven't written a book about him, neither have I written a book about myself. All I have done is translate into words – words he will probably never read; they are not intended for him – the way in which his existence has affected my life. An offering of a sort, bequeathed to others.

When I was a child, luxury was fur coats, evening dresses and villas by the sea. Later on, I thought it meant leading the life of an intellectual. Now I feel that it is also being able to live out a passion for a man or a woman.

ABOUT THE AUTHOR

ANNIE ERNAUX was born in 1940 in Normandy. She grew up in the small town of Yvetot, went to Rouen University, and then began to teach at the high school level. Currently a teacher of correspondence courses, she has two sons and lives outside of Paris. Her books have sold nearly a million copies in France, where they are taught in the schools as contemporary classics. Both of Ernaux's previous books, *A Woman's Story* and *A Man's Place*, were *New York Times* Notable Books of the Year. *A Woman's Story* was also a *Los Angeles Times* Fiction Prize finalist, and *A Man's Place* was a finalist for the French-American Translation Prize.